Careers without College

Paralegal

by Kathryn A. Quinlan

Content Consultant:
Marge Dover, CAE
Executive Director
National Association of Legal Assistants, Inc.

CAPSTONE
HIGH/LOW BOOKS
an imprint of Capstone Press

C A P S T O N E　　P R E S S

818 North Willow Street • Mankato, Minnesota 56001

http://www.capstone-press.com

Library of Congress Cataloging-in-Publication Data
Quinlan, Kathryn A.
　Paralegal / by Kathryn A. Quinlan.
　　p. cm. -- (Careers without college)
　Includes bibliographical references and index.
　ISBN 1-56065-706-5
　1. Legal assistants--Vocational guidance--United States.
I. Title. II. Series.
　KF320.L4Q56   1998
　340'.02373--dc21

97-35254
CIP
AC

Photo credits:
International Stock/Mark Bolster, 12; Patrick Ramsey, 4, 34; Johnny Stockshooter, 44
Photo Network, 26; Esbin-Anderson, cover; Bill Bachmann, 24; David Bentley, 9; Myrleen Ferguson, 17, 37; Dennis MacDonald, 32, 39
James L. Shaffer, 21, 23
Unicorn Stock Photos/Eric R. Berndt, 18; Steve Bourgeouis, 46; Jean Higgins, 11, 28; Gary L. Johnson, 6; Tom McCarthy, 15; Dick Young, 31, 43

Table of Contents

Fast Facts

Career Title	Paralegal
Minimum Educational Requirement	Some training after high school
Certification Requirement	Recommended
U.S. Salary Range	$18,000 to $50,000
Canadian Salary Range	$17,300 to $53,800 (Canadian dollars)
U.S. Job Outlook	Much faster than the average
Canadian Job Outlook	Much faster than the average
DOT Cluster (Dictionary of Occupational Titles)	Professional, technical, and managerial occupations
DOT Number	119.267-026
GOE Number (Guide for Occupational Exploration)	11.04.02
NOC (National Occupational Classification—Canada)	4211

Chapter 1

Job Responsibilities

Paralegals do some of the same work that lawyers do. A lawyer represents people in courts and in other legal situations. Paralegals work for lawyers. They help lawyers do their jobs.

Paralegals are also called legal assistants. They are important members of legal teams. Paralegals prepare background information for lawyers. But paralegals cannot do work that

Paralegals look up facts and do legal research.

7

requires a law degree. A degree is a title given by a college for completing a course of study. Paralegals cannot give legal advice or charge legal fees. They also cannot present cases in court.

On the Job

Paralegals work on cases. Cases are projects that lawyers work on for their clients. A client is a customer. Paralegals do some of the work on cases. This gives lawyers extra time to handle more difficult parts of cases.

Paralegals look up facts. Sometimes paralegals meet with clients. They often write reports about each case. These reports help lawyers get ready for court. Paralegals also answer clients' questions.

Most paralegals sort and store files for each case. The files hold documents. A document is a piece of paper that contains important information. Paralegals make sure that lawyers have all the documents they need for each case.

Paralegals find background information on cases.

Where Paralegals Work

Paralegals work in many settings. Some work for big companies such as banks and insurance companies. Others work for governments.

Most paralegals work in law firms. They play important roles on legal teams. These teams include lawyers, paralegals, and legal secretaries. Legal teams work as part of the judicial system. The judicial system is made up of courts, judges, and juries. A jury is a group of citizens that makes a decision based on evidence. Evidence is the information and facts that help lawyers prove something.

Many paralegals work in the court system. There are many kinds of courts. Some are local. Others are at the state or province level. Others are federal courts. Federal courts are at the national level. Some courts have trials. A trial is a court process that allows juries to decide if a charge or claim is true.

Paralegals work in many settings.

Chapter 2

What the Job Is Like

Paralegals work closely with lawyers and clients. They do many different jobs each day. Paralegals make sure lawyers have correct information about each case. They find this information by interviewing people. They also work with detectives and others to investigate cases. They report information to lawyers in writing.

Paralegals work with detectives and others to investigate cases.

Finding Witnesses

Paralegals find witnesses. A witness is a person who has seen or heard something about a case. Paralegals ask what witnesses know. Some witnesses offer important new facts about cases. Paralegals share these facts with lawyers.

Witnesses testify in court. Testify means to give evidence. Paralegals help lawyers decide what questions to ask witnesses.

Researching Cases

Paralegals look up information about former cases. These cases can set precedents. A precedent is a court decision from the past that judges and juries follow. A judge in a previous case may have said an action was illegal. The judge in a current case usually agrees with the previous judge. Lawyers and judges call this following precedent. Paralegals find precedents that help lawyers argue their cases.

Paralegals look up information about former cases.

14

CARLOS CASTANEDA
Ntozake Shange
Ridin' the Moon in Texas
THE PROPHET
KAHLIL GIBRAN
WEBSTER'S
NEW WORLD
DICTIONARY
of the
American
Language

Writing Summaries

Writing is an important skill for paralegals. Paralegals draft letters and legal documents. Lawyers use many kinds of legal documents in their work. Paralegals write the first drafts of some of these documents. Lawyers read and make changes to these documents.

Some lawyers ask paralegals to write case summaries. A summary gives the main points or ideas of a case. Paralegals meet clients. They find witnesses. They look up facts and precedents. Then they write what they have learned about each case. Summaries help lawyers prepare for court.

Some lawyers ask paralegals to write case summaries.

Chapter 3

Training

Paralegals must know a great deal about the law. Some paralegals receive training on the job. But most go through paralegal programs.

Paralegal Programs
Business schools offer the shortest paralegal programs. These can last from three to eighteen months. Many community or junior colleges offer two-year paralegal programs. Students in these

Many community or junior colleges offer two-year paralegal programs.

programs earn degrees. Degrees from two-year programs are associate's degrees. Some colleges offer four-year paralegal programs. Some students enter paralegal programs after earning four-year degrees in other fields.

People who want to be paralegals should ask paralegals and lawyers which programs are best. They can also ask paralegal groups. The American Association for Paralegal Education helps people choose good programs. The National Association of Legal Assistants also helps.

Classes

Most paralegal programs offer classes in law and legal methods. Legal methods are processes paralegals follow while doing legal work. Most programs teach students to do research. They also offer writing classes.

Most programs offer writing classes.

Many paralegal programs focus on ethics. An ethic is a belief in doing what is right. Lawyers and paralegals should have strong ethics.

Many paralegal programs offer classes in special areas of law. Some paralegals focus on one area. These paralegals are specialists. A specialist is a person who focuses on one area of work. Most paralegals learn to be specialists on the job. They become specialists through years of work and study.

Some students serve as interns. An intern learns a job by working with people already in the field. Paralegal interns work in law firms or courts for several weeks or months. They learn to work with lawyers. They gain experience inside courtrooms or law firms.

Certification Requirements

Some paralegals become certified legal assistants. Certified means to meet the standards of a state or province. The National Association of Legal

An intern learns a job by working with people already in the field.

Assistants (NALA) certifies legal assistants. Paralegals who pass NALA's two-day test become certified legal assistants. They can use the letters CLA after their names. Paralegals do not need to become certified legal assistants. But this title can help them find good jobs.

Exploring This Career

Students who want to be paralegals should work to get good grades. Students need good grades to get into good paralegal programs. Taking a wide range of classes is also helpful. Students should take English classes. Paralegals must be able to write and speak well. Computer classes are useful, too. Most paralegals use computers on the job.

Students can find out if they like legal work by getting part-time jobs. Many law firms hire young people to file papers and sort mail. Working at law firms allows students to talk to paralegals.

Most paralegals use computers on the job.

Personal Characteristics

Paralegals must be willing to work hard. They must be able to work quickly and meet deadlines. They also must be able to follow directions.

Paralegals spend many hours in law libraries. They read and report facts. They must enjoy doing research. They must be able to focus on details. Paralegals also must be able to think clearly. They must be able to share their thoughts with others.

Paralegals spend many hours in law libraries.

Chapter 4

Salary and Job Outlook

Paralegals work in many different places. Most work for law firms. But some paralegals work for courts or big companies. Paralegals earn from $18,000 to $50,000 per year. A paralegal's pay depends on many things.

Salary

Experienced paralegals usually make the most money. Paralegals who work in large cities

Paralegals who work for big law firms usually earn more money.

usually earn more money than those in smaller towns.

Paralegals who studied in good paralegal programs are more likely to find good jobs. Certified legal assistants earn more than workers without this title.

Paralegals also earn more money as they gain experience. Starting paralegals earn an average of $23,800. Paralegals who have worked for seven to ten years earn an average of $31,200. Those who have worked more than 10 years may earn more than $40,000 per year. Paralegals who supervise others can earn up to $50,000 per year. Some receive more money for working extra hours.

Benefits

Most paralegals receive paid holidays and paid sick days. Some paralegals also receive extra days off for working many hours.

Paralegals who have worked more than 10 years may earn more than $40,000 per year.

Some paralegals receive health insurance. Health insurance is protection from the costs of getting sick. People pay a small amount to insurance companies each month. The insurance companies will pay most of the bills if a person becomes sick.

Job Outlook

The paralegal field is growing. More and more law firms and companies are hiring paralegals. Paralegals help lawyers finish more work in less time. They help companies save money because they are less expensive to employ than lawyers. People who complete good programs and earn good grades find jobs as paralegals.

Paralegals help lawyers get more work done in less time.

Chapter 5

Where the Job Can Lead

Paralegals have many opportunities to advance. They can work in a certain area of the law. They can also become managers in law firms. Managers arrange schedules and assign tasks.

Advancement
Some paralegals advance by becoming specialists. Specialists can do many parts of a

Paralegals may talk to clients or ask witnesses questions.

lawyer's job. This way companies can save time and money because paralegals' salaries are lower then lawyers' salaries. Specialist paralegals have extra skills. They usually earn more money than other paralegals because they have more experience.

Paralegals who work in large law firms may manage other paralegals. They make sure everyone does a good job. Paralegals who manage other people earn more money.

Some paralegals choose to become lawyers. This requires receiving a college degree and attending law school. People who want to become lawyers also have to pass a test. This test is a bar examination.

Freelance Work

Some paralegals do freelance work. These paralegals work for many different lawyers and firms. They do not earn salaries. Instead

Paralegals who work in large law firms may manage other paralegals.

they receive money for each job they do. Freelance paralegals usually have a lot of experience. They are experts in certain areas of law. Lawyers hire them because they can work quickly and do good jobs. Freelance paralegals may charge more money for their work. But they usually do not receive paid holidays, paid sick time, or health insurance.

The best way to advance as a paralegal is to do good work. Paralegals who work hard usually advance quickly.

Freelance paralegals do work for many different lawyers and firms.

Words to Know

case (KAYSS)—a project that a lawyer works on for a client

certified (SUR-ti-fide)—to meet the standards of a state or province

client (KLY-uhnt)—a customer

document (DOK-yuh-muhnt)—a piece of paper that contains important information

draft (DRAFT)—a first copy of a piece of writing

evidence (EV-uh-duhnss)—information that helps lawyers prove something

health insurance (HELTH in-SHU-ruhnss)—protection from the costs of getting sick

lawyer (LOI-ur)—a person who represents people in courts and in other legal situations

precedent (PRESS-uh-duhnt)—a decision of the court from the past that judges and juries follow

research (REE-surch)—to study and learn about a subject

specialist (SPESH-uh-list)—a person who focuses on one area of work

trial (TRYE-uhl)—the court process to decide if a charge or claim is true

witness (WIT-niss)—a person who has seen or heard something about a case

To Learn More

Bernardo, Barbara. *Paralegal: An Insider's Guide to One of the Fastest-Growing Careers.* Princeton, N.J.: Peterson's Guides, 1993.

Estrin, Chere B. *Paralegal Career Guide.* New York: Wiley Law Publications, 1996.

Fins, Alice. *Opportunities in Paralegal Careers.* Lincolnwood, Ill.: VGM Career Horizons, 1990.

Wagner, Andrea. *How to Land Your First Paralegal Job: An Insider's Guide to the Fastest-Growing Profession of the New Millennium.* Upper Saddle River, N.J.: Prentice Hall, 1998.

Useful Addresses

American Association for Paralegal Education
PO Box 40244
Overland Park, KS 66204

National Association of Legal Assistants
1516 South Boston Avenue, Suite 200
Tulsa, OK 74119

National Federation of Paralegal Associations
PO Box 33108
Kansas City, MO 64114-0108

National Paralegal Association
PO Box 406
Solebury, PA 18963

Internet Sites

American Bar Association Home Page
http://www.abanet.org

National Association of Legal Assistants
http://www.nala.org

National Federation of Paralegal Associations
http://www.paralegals.org

Paralegal and Related Occupations
http://workinfonet.bc.ca/workfutures/text/
  body/4211eb_t.htm

Paralegals
http://stats.bls.gov/oco/ocos114.htm

Index